Fantastic Flora

THE WORLD'S BIGGEST, BADDEST, AND SMELLIEST PLANTS

...

Ann McCallum Staats

illustrated by Zoë Ingram

≡ mit Kids Press

The MIT Press, the ≡**mit Kids** Press colophon, and MIT Kids Press
are trademarks of The MIT Press, a department of the Massachusetts
Institute of Technology, and used under license from The MIT Press.
The colophon and MIT Kids Press are registered in the
US Patent and Trademark Office.

First edition 2025

Library of Congress Control Number: pending
ISBN 978-1-5362-3283-7

CCP 30 29 28 27 26 25
10 9 8 7 6 5 4 3 2 1

Printed in Shenzhen, Guangdong, China

This book was typeset in Chaparral Pro and Neue Kabel.
The illustrations were created digitally.

MIT Kids Press
an imprint of Candlewick Press
99 Dover Street
Somerville, Massachusetts 02144

mitkidspress.com
candlewick.com

EU Authorized Representative: HackettFlynn Ltd., 36 Cloch Choirneal,
Balrothery, Co. Dublin, K32 C942, Ireland. EU@walkerpublishinggroup.com

CONTENTS

THE SMELLY

THE EXCEPTIONALLY STRANGE

Introduction

Rumble. It's the sound of your stomach begging for food. You might wander into the kitchen to grab a snack. *Brrr.* It's your body shivering when the temperature drops. Maybe you snuggle into a sweater. But what about plants? When the going gets tough, plants don't have the same options as us humans. They need a savvy way to survive in all kinds of conditions. Limited nutrients. The coldest cold, the driest dry. Cracks in sidewalks. Murky water or a moderate fire. Pests that want to eat them to death.

When plants face a problem, it's not like they can run away or pack up and move somewhere else. That's why plants thrive using brilliant—and bizarre—adaptations. They use these features to help them succeed no matter what the environment throws at them. Some have thorns to discourage hungry predators. Others scam their way close to helpful pollinators so they can reproduce. Some ask for insect assistance using chemical signals. Wherever you look, plants are masters at survival.

With a focus on some of the biggest, the baddest, the smelliest, and the strangest plants around the globe, the facts you'll encounter may seem a little . . . unnatural. They're not. Plants can't talk or walk and don't have a brain protected inside a bony skull, but they've figured out how to flourish.

In this book, you'll meet plants that eat meat and one, dead horse arum, that pretends to *be* meat—with a smell of rotten flesh that's so rank you'll want to plug your nose. Crane your neck back to marvel at plants taller than a twenty-story building; crouch down to unearth plants smaller than your toenail. Find out how—and why—certain plants live for centuries or generate enough heat to melt snow. Uncover bold vegetation that disguises itself to look like something else. Have you ever seen plants that look like stones?

As you leaf through this book, you'll discover the wildest plant traits. Exploding seeds. Fireproof trunks. Deadly berries. Adaptations so strange you'll need to know more. Get ready to dig into the sensational science of plant survival!

THE
BIG

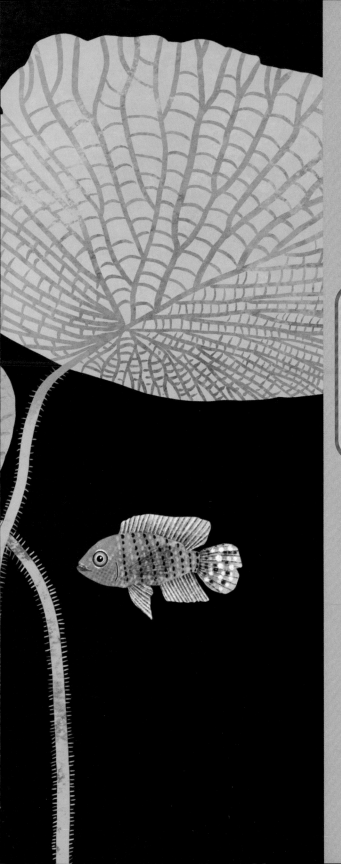

Chapter 1
SUPERSIZE LEAF

If you're looking for a place to sit, try the Bolivian water lily—it's strong enough to support a human.

It's a hot, sunny day and the water is sparkling. At least, it would sparkle if the sun could reach it. Underneath a dense ceiling of supersize Bolivian water-lily leaves on the river's surface, the light is gloomy, making algae and water plants scarce. A fish swims by, hungry and hunting for food. There's not much vegetation to eat . . . aside from the lily. The fish draws closer, intent on taking a chomp out of the Bolivian water lily's tasty stalk, the only thing holding the plant to the river's bottom. Without this anchor, the lily will rot and die.

But the Bolivian water lily is NOT a favorite fish food. Large and in charge, the underwater section of the plant is protected with a kind of anti-fish armor. Thorny barbs coat the stalk and bottom surface of the water lily. If any hungry predators do try to cozy up for a snack, they'll soon find out that it's a losing battle. Is Bolivian water lily delicious? Probably. But ouch? Absolutely.

Native to northeast Bolivia, this plant's scientific name is *Victoria boliviana*; Bolivian water lily is its common name. There are two other closely related giant water-lily species found nearby: *Victoria amazonica*, which has a local nickname, *auapé-yaponna*, after a bird that rests on its enormous leaves, and *Victoria cruziana*, which is sometimes called *yrupe*, or "water plate." Indigenous peoples have found practical uses for these plants. The ground-up seeds can make a terrific substitute for maize. And the roots? Their black pigment makes an excellent hair dye.

Each Bolivian water-lily leaf is anchored to the river bottom by a stalk that's up to 26 feet (8 meters) long—about as tall as four refrigerators stacked on top of each other. The floating leaves are green on top, where they're exposed to the sun, and red underneath. Since there's little sunlight underwater, the leaf undersides don't contain **chlorophyll**, the green compound responsible for absorbing energy from the sun. Each leaf is shaped like an upturned bottlecap—but WAY bigger. This plant is the world's largest lily and holds the record for the biggest simple leaf in the world.

How big is big? Each floating leaf of the Bolivian water lily grows up to 10 feet (3 meters) across. And these leaves grow *fast*—up to 20 inches (50 centimeters) in one day. That's as long as six crayons. But what's the point of getting so large? Is there an advantage to being so gigantic?

In the plant world, it's all about survival. The Bolivian water lily wants to collect the maximum amount of sunlight to help in the process of making food, but it doesn't want to spend too much energy doing it. It's like shopping for a new bike. You want the best bike for the lowest price. As each Bolivian water-lily leaf grows larger, it has a greater surface to absorb energy-giving sunlight. Because each leaf floats, it's a low-energy way of supporting something big, and big in this case means better. There's another side benefit to having such a giant size. The Bolivian water lily does a good job squeezing out plant competitors. It uses strength and size to get rivals to "bud" out!

While the Bolivian water lily's leaves are fantastic, they shouldn't get all the attention. Its flowers are pretty spectacular, too. But observe quickly. The flowers have a life cycle of just two days before they sink below the water's surface. On the first day, a bright

A SIMPLE THING ABOUT LEAVES

When you want to talk about leaves, it's simple . . . or compound. Simple leaves have undivided **blades** called laminae that come in different shapes and sizes. They have a middle vein and edges that may be smooth, wavy, or jagged like a saw. Simple leaves are attached one by one to the rest of the plant directly or via a supporting stalk, the **petiole**. Examine the simple leaves on a maple or mango tree, for instance. Compare those with compound leaves, which are made up of more than one leaflet. A collection of leaves grows from a central stalk, which then connects to the stem of the plant. For example, you'd have super good luck if you found a four-leaf clover, but a three-leaf clover has a compound leaf system, too.

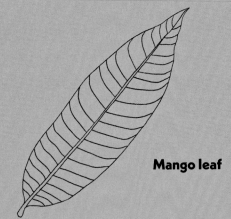

Mango leaf

white flower blooms at dusk and emits a sweet-smelling perfume. Some people say it smells like pineapple. Flying beetles agree that these flowers are quite lovely. Attracted to the color and smell, the insects travel from one flower to the next, helping to transfer **pollen** that becomes stuck to their bodies. But there's a catch . . .

Or rather, a trap. Once the beetle flies into the flower, the petals close over the insect, temporarily caging it in. (Luckily for the beetles, there's plenty of **nectar** to eat while they're stuck inside.) As the insect bumps around trying to escape, pollen from its previous travels gets knocked off. Now it's time for the Bolivian water lily to get to work. Using the transferred pollen from the beetle, the flower matures and turns from white to

sunlight

carbon dioxide

water

oxygen

FOOD THROUGH PHOTOSYNTHESIS

Plants create food for themselves in a process called **photosynthesis**. The recipe includes water, carbon dioxide, and sunlight. The plant collects water, mostly from soil (if it's a land plant). It pulls carbon dioxide, a gas that's toxic to animals in large doses, from the air. To harvest energy from the sun, the plant uses chlorophyll, which is found in the green parts of the plant. Now it's time to get cooking. Each leaf produces nutrition—mostly a kind of sugar called glucose—for the plant. Some of this is used right away and some is stored for later. A huge benefit to humans and other animals is that the by-product of photosynthesis, oxygen, is released back into the air. When plants remove excess carbon dioxide and replace it with oxygen, they clean the air and make it possible for us to breathe. Ahhh, take a deep breath and thank a plant today!

pink. Duty done, the flower opens to release the beetle and then sinks underwater where it produces a seed, carefully encased in a bubble of air. When it's time, the seed floats away and later falls into the mud to grow the next beautiful Bolivian water lily.

Be-LEAF It or Not

If the Bolivian water lily is so huge, how can it stay afloat?

With its ribbed mega-construction, of course. Thick ridges radiate from the center of the leaf's underwater surface. The ridges form boxed sections that trap air and help the leaf float. In 1851, in London, England, the Crystal Palace was constructed from glass using the same design principles as this leaf. It was one of the first examples of **biomimicry**, when people take ideas from nature and apply them to solve human challenges. It goes to show you how much we can learn from plants.

WATER WORLD

While many plants prefer firm ground, the Bolivian water lily is one of countless others that make their home in water. The largest plant in the world, *Posidonia australis*, is a water plant, too. It gets its first name from Poseidon, the ancient Greek god of the sea. Its second name refers to where it's located, a large swath of ocean off the coast of southern Australia. When scientists first studied this patch of seagrass, they didn't realize it was just one plant. After all, it spread over 70 square miles (180 square kilometers). (Think of how long it would take to swim such a great distance when the record for swimming just ONE mile is about fifteen minutes!) But the plant had one root system, and, understanding that the plant grew 14 inches (36 centimeters) per year, scientists were able to figure out that it's more than 4,500 years old. For thousands of years, the ribbon-shaped plant has supported fish and other wild-life. It has helped filter the water and hold the seabed in place. *Posidonia australis* also releases valuable oxygen. Today, scientists are working to preserve this important plant and protect it from threats such as the changing climate, various storms, and human interaction.

Chapter 2
FAN-TASTIC
AND GIGANTIC

This plant has blue seed covers
and a spread of leaves shaped
like the fan of a peacock's tail—
if the peacock were as tall as
three basketball hoops.

Lost and alone, a weary traveler turns in a circle to see if anything looks familiar. It doesn't. Will she wander for hours, walking first one way and then the other, until, exhausted and thirsty, she finally stumbles upon home? If only she had a compass . . .

Maybe she does! Found naturally in humid areas on the world's fourth-largest island, traveler's palm looks like a giant fan—or a display of peacock feathers. And there's something curious about

WHAT'S IN A NAME?

People often call plants by their nicknames or by a common name, but depending on where you live and who you talk to, there might be multiple names for one plant. Scientists weed out the confusion by assigning official names to every plant. We can thank Carolus Linnaeus, who set up a two-part naming system in 1707 using Latin, the modern international language of science. The first word in a plant's name refers to its **genus**, the group of plant it belongs to. The second part of the name indicates a species and sometimes also points to a defining feature. The scientific name for traveler's palm is *Ravenala madagascariensis*. *Ravenala* comes from a Malagasy word that means "forest leaves," and *madagascariensis* refers to its country of origin, Madagascar.

the way the plant grows. The rounded pattern of the leaves is often oriented east to west, which could help the traveler find her way home.

At least, that's one rumor about where traveler's palm got its common name. Here's another theory: since rainwater often collects in pockets at the base of the plant's leaves, the plant can provide an emergency source of drinking water. Hmmm, maybe. But travelers should beware of unclean water.

Look up. Way up. Traveler's palm grows up to 30 feet (9 meters) tall, about half the length of a bowling lane. Notice the twenty or more leaves on a full-grown plant—each one up to 15 feet (4.5 meters) long. As a new leaf unfurls, it pushes against its neighbors, ultimately forming a unique semicircular crown. Each mature leaf is held up by a sturdy stem, the petiole. On the leaf blade, veins run at right angles from the central **midrib** found in the middle of the leaf. Whenever there's a strong wind—often—the leaves tear along these veins. But this shredded appearance isn't a bad thing. Sure, it makes the leaves look a little messy, but the flapping leaves and smaller surface area of each leaf helps the plant by reducing excessive heat. Phew!

Traveler's palm shares its home with plenty of unique plants and animals. On the island of Madagascar, 90 percent of the plants and animals can't be found naturally anywhere else on Earth. This includes small, furry lemurs, mammals that love to slurp nectar from the flowers on the traveler's

WHAT CLUES CAN YOU FIND IN THESE PLANT NAMES?

Juniperus horizontalis (creeping juniper)
Rhus aromatica (fragrant sumac)
Magnolia virginiana (sweet bay magnolia)

If you came up with the words *horizontal*, *aroma* or *aromatic*, and *Virginia*, well done! These are descriptive terms for each of these plants.

Sweet bay magnolia

palm. These pale blooms sprout from a green covering called a **bract**—a narrow casing that looks like a boat. When black-and-white ruffed lemurs feast on the nectar from the traveler's palm, the plant gets something in return. The animals break open the tree's flowers, and pollen attaches to their snout and fur.

Lemurs also act as seed dispensers for the traveler's palm, transporting the seeds to new places to grow. The seeds, encased in an edible, bright blue covering called an **aril**, attract the animals with their unusual color. Lemurs eat the seeds and then poop them out in another location. This happens fast because the seeds contain a laxative, a substance that helps them move quickly through the lemur's

stigma

anther

ovary

ATTRACTIVE FLOWERS: THE PROCESS OF POLLINATION

In nature, plants work to create plenty of offspring. Those with flowers rely on a clever process that starts with pollination. The plant needs to transfer pollen dust from one part of the flower, the **anther**, to another part of the flower, the **stigma**. It's how fertilization occurs, which creates a seed. There are two types of fertilization: **self-pollination** and **cross-pollination**. Self-pollinating plants take care of this system themselves—no help necessary, thank you. In cross-pollination, insects, birds, other animals (sometimes including humans), or even wind or water help transport the powdery pollen of one plant to another plant in the same species. There, the pollen falls off, passing onto the stigma. Now the plant can start the process of reproduction. The tiny pollen grains travel to the plant's **ovary**, the place where seeds form.

digestive system (which ensures that the seeds stay intact). The height of traveler's palm is a win-win situation: It helps keep the lemurs safe from ground predators when they're high up in the tree. And by ensuring lemur safety, traveler's palm gets the benefit of pollen and seed transportation.

🍃 Be-LEAF It or Not
Is traveler's palm actually a palm tree?

No! It's a trick question. Traveler's palm might have *palm* in its name, but it's actually no palm at all. Think of it like a friendly nickname, a common label that people simply got used to using. Real palm trees yield fruits such as coconuts and dates, while traveler's palm produces capsules with seeds inside. Traveler's palm is part of the bird-of-paradise family and is related to ginger and banana plants. Keep in mind, though, that it's the biggest of the bunch.

HERE TO THERE:
Seed Dispersal

No arms, no legs, and no trains, planes, or cars, either. But that doesn't mean that a plant's offspring can't spread from one location to another. If you've ever seen dandelions scattered throughout a lawn or park, you'll understand that plant seeds have developed fascinating ways to travel. Parent plants want to help their seeds find the best place to start growing, usually away from themselves. Why squabble over space, water, and the soil's nutrients?

Plants help their seeds disperse in different ways. Some seeds have feathery attachments that allow them to float in the wind. Others, like tulips or maple trees, have seed holders that flutter in the air. Water can also help. Coconut seeds might spend months floating at sea before finding some land to settle on. Mangrove trees, growing near water, use waterways to disperse their seeds, too. And have you ever wondered how having delicious fruit is useful for plants? These plants count on animals eating their fruit. When the animal swallows the seeds along with the fruit, they poop the seeds out later—and help new plants grow in different locations. And while you might consider it a nuisance if you come home with burrs or spines attached to your clothing after walking through a field, plants like burdock have seeds that have adapted to hook onto clothing or an animal's fur to hitch a ride to a new growing location.

GIANT SEQUOIA

Sequoiadendron giganteum

NATURAL HABITAT:

Sierra Nevada range,
in California

Chapter 3
A LONG WAY UP

Sequoia National Park was the
first US national park established
to protect a tree—the mighty
giant sequoia.

Crackle. Hiss. Flames sizzle as they consume branches, shrubs, and debris along the forest floor. As the fire grows, it engulfs whole trees, jumping from one branch to another. Nearby is a grove of giant sequoias, some thousands of years old. Will the flames spell disaster for these trees that are older than the invention of paper?

No, just the opposite. For the giant sequoia, a moderate forest fire is a good thing. It helps the tree reproduce, and here's how: Giant sequoias are **conifers**, which means their seeds develop inside **cones**. Sequoia cones grow high in the tree, where they're safe from the fire itself. But the fire's heat makes the air hot enough for them

C IS FOR CONE

The majority of trees are either conifers or **deciduous trees**. One way to remember the difference is to think of **c**onifers as having **c**ones. A cone is a seed home, where a conifer tree grows and stores its seeds. Another difference is that most conifers have needles or scales instead of leaves. They are evergreens, which means that they stay green throughout the year. If C is for **c**one and **c**onifer, D is for **d**eciduous, **d**rop, and **d**ormant. Most deciduous trees have green leaves, but these turn various colors when the weather gets cooler. They *drop* off in the autumn, leaving the tree *dormant*, or inactive, throughout the winter months. Deciduous trees grow new leaves in the spring, and the process starts over.

Sequoia cone

to dry out so they can release their seeds. This takes some time, which works in the tree's favor. By the time the seeds fall to the earth, the fire has passed by.

Once on the ground, the seeds of the giant sequoia are covered by a helpful layer of nutritious, leftover ash from the recent fire. On the newly cleared forest floor—the understory—sprouting new giant sequoias don't have to compete for sunlight or the best water and soil. It spells success for the seeds, but what about the tree itself? What does it do to keep from getting scorched to death while the fire rages?

De-FENSE! As a giant sequoia matures, smaller, lower branches fall off. On a mature tree, the branches grow high on the trunk—far from the threat of a ground fire. Down at ground level, the trunk has its own protection. Up to 2 feet (60 centimeters) thick, the soft, reddish-brown bark contains a chemical called tannic acid, which not only resists fire but also deters insects and disease. Even with all these defenses, in some circumstances a giant sequoia can still catch on fire. For example, if there's ever a lightning strike to the crown of the tree (the topmost branches and leaves), it may burst into flame. But it can still survive. A giant sequoia can repair the damage and regrow, even if the fire continues to burn for some time before it rains or the fire dies out. It's no wonder these trees live as long as they do!

Giant sequoias grow naturally in only one place on Earth: a narrow strip of land on the western slopes of the Sierra Nevada range, in California. You'll find the trees

TAKING THEIR TIME

Seeds wait to germinate—or develop—until conditions are just right. For some seeds, there is no rush. In 1967, scientists discovered a cache of Arctic lupine seeds more than ten thousand years old that were still able to sprout. In 2007, a team of researchers found preserved seeds in an ancient squirrel's burrow in Siberia, which they were later able to grow. The seeds were thirty-two thousand years old! Under normal circumstances, seeds don't wait that long before they start the process of germination. Many take days or weeks to germinate, though some fruit trees can wait for years until their seeds begin to sprout. Giant sequoia cones, which each have about two hundred seeds inside, remain on the tree for up to twenty years. When finally released from the cone, few seeds live long enough to grow into trees (most plants produce lots of seeds, which increases the chances of a few of them sprouting).

partway up the side of these mountains. Giant sequoias prefer a specific altitude where there's snow in the winter but it's not too hot or dry in the summer. When you need at least 500 gallons (1,900 liters) of water *per day* to survive, especially during periods of active growth in the summer, melted snow and moist conditions are a huge help.

Giant sequoias aren't the tallest trees on Earth, but by volume, they're the largest. When conditions are right, they grow quickly, seeking out better sunlight as they expand upward and away from other competing shrubs and trees. The biggest of them is a superstructure named General Sherman, a mind-boggling 275 feet (84 meters) tall with an estimated mass of 2.7 million pounds (1.2 million kilograms)—about the weight of two hundred elephants or eleven blue whales. If you tried to circle the bottom of its trunk with a length of string, you'd need a piece longer than a basketball court (103 feet/31 meters). And underground? A mature giant sequoia's root system can stretch more than 150 feet (46 meters) from the base. These trees are so colossal that people have driven cars through them, built a dance floor on a stump, and carved a fallen log into a house. It's easy to feel like a toothpick when you're standing next to a giant sequoia.

Giant sequoias take a long time to get gigantic. General Sherman is approximately 2,200 years old. Other trees are even older. Grizzly Giant is about 3,000 years old, and the President is around 3,200. The

Muir Snag—no longer living—
was about 3,500 years old when
it died.

But how can scientists mea-
sure how old a tree is? When it
comes to an ancient sequoia,
for example, it's not like there's
anyone still alive who could
tell you when they noticed it
first growing. One way to calcu-
late the age of a tree is through
dendrochronology (*dendro*
means "tree" in Greek, and
chronology refers to the study
of time). Dendrochronologists
study the pattern of growth rings
on a tree. As a tree grows, the
trunk thickens, quickly at first
and then more slowly as it ages.
You can count these markers of
new growth on the cross sections
of most trees.

There's definitely some-
thing otherworldly about giant

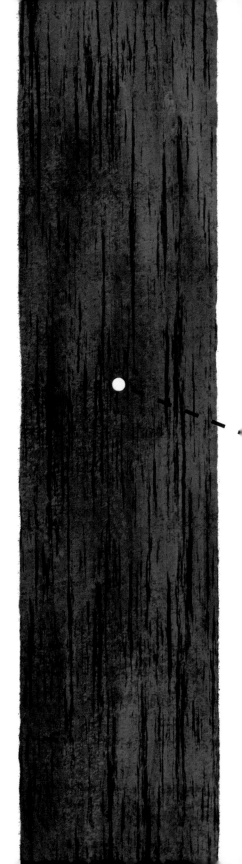

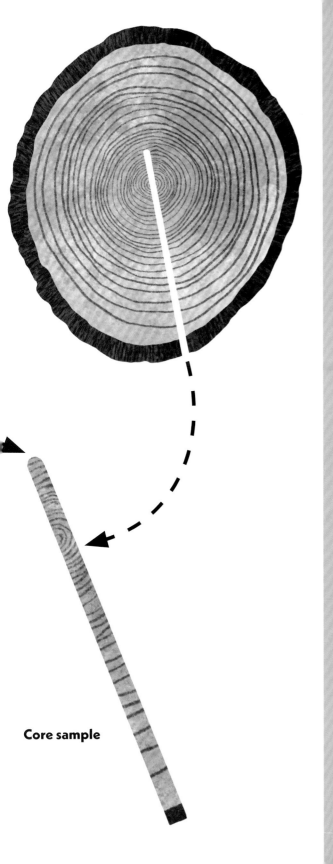

Core sample

BORING A TREE—
NOT AT ALL BORING

Scientists know how to collect data from living trees like their age and growth history without causing the trees harm. To do so, they use a tool called an increment borer. The tool drills horizontally into a tree and pulls out a straw-shaped sample of wood about a quarter inch in diameter. To prevent disease or further injury to the tree, the dendrochronologist then fills in the tiny hole in the tree. Next, they study the core sample. Each tree shows a series of early and late wood rings. Early wood rings develop during quick growing times, the spring and early summer. Late wood rings are dark, narrow bands from when the tree was growing slowly. Each pair of early and late wood rings shows one year's worth of growth. During an ideal year when there was plenty of water and nutrients, this growth ring is wider than during a period of drought or less favorable conditions.

sequoias. They might make you feel like you've landed in the pages of *Alice in Wonderland* or in a science fiction movie. Of course, those are fictional stories. The next time you want to feel truly tiny, go for a hike through a grove of giant sequoias—physically or online. Prepare to feel very, very small!

 ## Be-LEAF It or Not

Are giant sequoias the oldest trees on the planet?

No! They're old, but not the oldest. In Iran, a cypress tree known as Sarv-e Abarkuh is estimated to be more than 4,000 years old. A Great Basin bristle-cone pine named Methuselah, growing in Inyo National Forest in California, is thought to be more than 4,800 years old. And if you're in Chile, you can visit an alerce tree named Gran Abuelo (meaning great-grandfather in Spanish), recently estimated to be even older, possibly more than 5,000 years old!

THE UNDEAD:
Starting with a Seed

And now for a little math: moisture + warmth + oxygen = signal to start growing.

A baby plant within a seed is called an **embryo**. The seed also contains a supply of plant food to get things started. This provides enough energy for the seed to sprout and eventually grow into a plant that can sustain itself. When a seed is ready to sprout, most plants produce a root. This new growth "roots" around the soil, usually growing down while looking for water. Then, shoot! A sprout pokes up and produces new growth above ground. Soon, leaves spring open. Good thing, too, because the leaves need to produce food ASAP for the plant through photosynthesis. This energy helps it grow. But not all seeds look or act the same. The tiniest seeds are like specks of dust. Orchids produce millions of these in hopes that at least some will sprout. Coco-de-mer, a kind of palm tree, has the largest seed, an extraordinary 40 or more pounds (18 kilograms or more). That's as heavy as a 5-gallon (19-liter) bucket of water filled to the top! The next time you gaze at a tree, bush, or flower, consider its humble beginning, the seed that started it all.

THE BAD

DEADLY NIGHTSHADE

Atropa belladonna

NATURAL HABITAT:

Europe, North Africa, and areas of the Middle East

Chapter 4
IN THE DEAD OF THE NIGHT

Enemies beware! Throughout history, people have used this infamous plant's poison to commit murder.

In ancient Greece, people believed that everyone's life was controlled by three divine beings called the Fates. Clotho spun each person's thread of life at birth, and Lachesis measured how many ups and downs each person would have. Finally—SNIP!—Atropa cut the thread when she determined it was time to die. Here's the connection: this deadly plant's first name is *Atropa*, too . . .

Meet *Atropa belladonna*, otherwise known as deadly nightshade. No matter what you call it, this plant has some lethal characteristics. Its serious side effects are a form of plant defense, a way to persuade animals to move on. To many creatures, including humans, all parts of the plant are poisonous, but the roots, leaves, and ripe berries are especially dangerous. For young children, chowing down on just two or three berries can be fatal; for adults, as few as ten can kill. Symptoms include a racing heart, hallucinations,

ANIMALS BEWARE! POISONOUS PLANTS AHEAD

Redness. Swelling. Blisters. And, oh, the itch! There's a reason we include the word *poison* in the names for poison ivy, poison oak, and poison sumac. But while humans learn to avoid toxic plants, how do animals know what to stay away from? They can't check in a book or online! Instead, animals learn to be cautious. An unpleasant smell and taste might stop them from eating something. Or they may try a small amount of a plant first to see if there are any problems. They might mix things up—eat a bit of this and a bit of that—to counteract the poison. Or, with their unique body chemistry, different animals may be able to tolerate different plants. As for belladonna, it can be fatal for humans, cats, and dogs, but horses, rabbits, sheep, goats, pigs, and slugs dine on this plant with no problems.

Poison ivy

and seizures—which can lead to death. Even touching belladonna can trigger a rash. This plant is a good reminder to never meddle with things you find growing in nature that you can't identify—it might not turn out well.

Surprisingly, *Atropa belladonna* comes from a respectable family. It's related to potatoes, tomatoes, eggplants, and chili peppers. But, as belladonna matures, it becomes more and more toxic. Belladonna poisoning leads to various symptoms. To remember these, medical professionals think of the mnemonic "Hot as a hare, blind as a bat, dry as a bone, red as a beet, and mad as a hen." In other words, victims might experience a fever, blindness, a dry mouth and throat, flushed cheeks, and severe mental confusion.

But *Atropa belladonna* isn't all

bad. The second part of its scientific name, *belladonna*, means beautiful lady. During the Italian Renaissance (from about 1300 to 1600 CE), Italian women used tiny extracts from the plant to add a blush to their cheeks and to dilate their pupils. Back then, having large pupils was a fashion statement.

Aside from makeup, in the right dosage, belladonna has been beneficial in medicine, too. Before modern healthcare, people had to rely on natural remedies. Since belladonna can induce a coma, this was a great solution—if you were extremely careful—when a doctor had to perform surgery. In modern times, doctors conducting eye exams can dilate a patient's eye using a solution containing *atropine*, a chemical found naturally in belladonna. This helps the doctor see inside the eye more easily.

DEATH BY PLANT!

Belladonna is sometimes referred to as the drug of assassins. Since ancient times, people have used it to poison their enemies. The early Roman army dipped arrow tips in a paste made from the plant to make their weapons even more lethal. Others died after consuming deadly drinks or food poisoned with belladonna. For example, as (bad) luck would have it, the Roman emperor Augustus may have died from belladonna poisoning. It was rumored that Livia, his wife, wanted her son to become emperor, so she poisoned her husband to get him out of the way. Some say that Agrippina the Younger did the same thing to her husband, Emperor Claudius, though she had another woman, Locusta, carry out her scheme. It makes sense that many wealthy people in ancient Rome (and other parts of the world) had tasters try their food first to make sure it wasn't poisoned.

What does this sometimes-helpful, sometimes-hurtful plant look like? Found in damp, shady areas, the plant grows up to 7 feet (2.1 meters) tall. With pretty, bell-shaped purple flowers and shiny black berries, it's tempting to take a closer look. Don't. Leave it to the experts and run, don't walk, from this deadly plant.

Be-LEAF It or Not

Do foods that we eat have toxic parts?

Yes—there are plenty of delicious foods that have toxic parts. When you bite into a crisp, cool apple, maybe you munch on a little poison along with the delicious fruit. Wait! *Poison?* Yes, but there's no need to worry, and here's why. Apple seeds contain a toxic chemical called amygdalin. Luckily for us, these seeds have a protective covering that keeps the poison from being absorbed into the body, so eating a few isn't going to hurt you. Other popular foods have toxic parts, too. Potatoes and tomatoes? They have poisonous leaves, roots, and stems. Rhubarb? Steer clear of the leaves.

PLANT LOVE— What Does a Botanist Do?

"Plants are amazing organisms! People forget that every aspect of our lives is dependent upon plants: air, food, water, medicine, etc., etc., etc.!!"
—Dr. Tanisha Williams, founder of *Black Botanists Week*

Botanists are plant scientists, and they work in a variety of different fields (that is, career fields!). They might have jobs at a botanical garden, at an arboretum, in a laboratory, or with the forest service. Some botanists figure out ways to cultivate certain crops to make food more nutritious or easier to grow and manage. Others work on the science of plant medicine. With *Atropa belladonna*, today's scientists have extracted chemicals that, alone or combined with others, help with issues such as motion sickness or controlling heart rate. Botanists also look to plants for alternative, cleaner fuel sources. A biotechnologist, one type of botany specialist, works in a lab and conducts experiments with plants. Take plastic, most of which is made from petroleum. Biotechnologists today are exploring ways to produce the best biodegradable plastics using renewable plant sources. These will be easier on the environment and won't pile up in landfills because they'll break down naturally. Who knows what plant mysteries botanists will uncover next?

SANDBOX TREE

Hura crepitans

NATURAL HABITAT:

Tropical regions of Central and South America

Chapter 5
PLANT WITH A BANG

With vicious prickles and explosive seeds, this plant is dynamite—literally.

The sun blazes down. It's quiet, too, as most animals are resting in the heat of the day. Suddenly, *BOOM!* The blast is followed by a bang, first one and then more. What is it? Did someone let off a firecracker . . . or maybe a series of bombs?

There's a reason why some people call this the dynamite tree, though it's more commonly called the sandbox tree. Either way, *Hura crepitans* gets its reputation from a process called **dehiscence**, when mature fruit spontaneously splits or bursts open. With the sandbox tree, this happens when its pumpkin-shaped fruit ripens and dries out. Each fruit capsule, 3–4 inches (7.5–10 centimeters) in diameter, starts out green. As it dehydrates, the fruit turns

THE PRESSURE'S ON

In nature, plants rely on various schemes to disperse their seeds. With ballistic seed dispersal, seeds hurtle from the parent plant in order to find new, fresh areas to grow. The sandbox tree isn't the only one to expel its seeds in such a forceful manner. Take the squirting cucumber. Instead of drying out like the sandbox tree's fruit, water builds up inside the plant. Suddenly, a stream of seeds shoots from the spot where the cucumber was once attached to the stalk. Other plants that use ballistic seed dispersal include kapok trees, okra, Mexican petunia, and the aptly named firecracker plant.

Squirting cucumber

brown, and the stress builds. In a sudden, explosive movement, the capsule ruptures and, if there are no obstacles in the way, flings seeds up to 60 feet (18 meters) away. The force of the blast is so intense that scientists have recorded a seed speed of up to 150 miles (241 kilometers) per hour, twice as fast as a car driving on the highway.

So why call it the sandbox tree, then, which sounds so tame and fun? According to early sources, its fruit pods were once turned into pounce pots, important tools for writing. Sawed in half—emptied of seeds and *not* about to explode—the pods made dishes that were perfect for holding the sand used in old-fashioned penmanship. Before modern pens were available, people dipped an instrument into ink when they wanted to write. To clean up excess blotches of ink, they sprinkled a little sand (or other powder) onto the paper and then dusted it off. There you have it, though it seems like a stretch to name an entire tree species after this practice.

Located near the edges or cleared areas of tropical rain forests, mostly in Central and South America, the sandbox tree grows 100 feet (30.5 meters) tall or more, with fruit high in its branches. It's a member of the Euphorbiaceae family. Others in the family include the rubber tree, poinsettia, and cassava. Compared to these peaceful relatives, some might consider the sandbox tree the "bad apple" of the family—and not just because of its catapulting seeds.

Sandbox tree seed capsule

The sandbox tree's smooth, gray-green trunk is covered in sharp prickles. Each of these spikes is around an inch or more long and has a needle-like tip, giving this tree another fitting nickname: the monkey-no-climb tree. With these razor barbs covering the trunk, it would be extremely unpleasant to clamber up.

With the sandbox tree, the danger continues. The seeds are highly toxic to humans and can cause vomiting, diarrhea, and cramping. No, thanks. But it's not just the seeds that should be avoided. The sap is also poisonous. Contact with it can cause a rash and, if it gets into your eyes, blindness. When people use the wood in construction or to make furniture, they carefully drain the sap from the wood first.

As with many plants, the sandbox tree also has several

A THORN IN THEIR SIDE

Often people use the terms *thorn*, *spine*, and *prickle* interchangeably, but there's a difference. Thorns are a modified stem or branch, and they contain systems to transport nutrition and water within the plant. They can be one long needle, or they can divide into two or more. Wild citrus trees or hawthorn shrubs have thorns. Spines, however, are modified leaf structures. The edges of the leaf may have spines or the whole leaf might be a spine—a cactus is a good example. Not only does a cactus spine dissuade animals from taking a bite, but it also helps provide shade to the plant in the scorching temperatures of the desert. On the other hand, prickles, like the ones on a rose or the sandbox tree, are a sharp outgrowth from the stem or bark. Thorn, spine, or prickle, the upshot is the same: painful protuberances save the plant from animals that might otherwise nibble it to death.

Prickly pear cactus

useful features—as long as you know what you're doing. Oil from the seeds makes a good laxative, which helps expel waste. In the right dose, oil from the leaves helps with skin issues like eczema or for relieving some of the symptoms of joint swelling and pain. And in the past, the sap was handy for making poison arrows.

 # Be-LEAF It or Not

How else has the sandbox tree been helpful to humans?

Long ago, Indigenous peoples, such as the Yawanawá of Bolivia, found a clever way to use the sandbox tree to collect dinner. They crushed together the poisonous parts, including the bark. They then dropped this mash into a loosely woven basket, which they swirled through a small pond or sectioned-off area of water. The poison stunned a catch of fish, making them easy to gather with a net or by hand. Luckily, once cooked, the fish could be eaten with no ill effect.

UP NEXT:
Sappy Science

Sap, the often-sticky fluid that sometimes leaks from trees, is the lifeblood of a tree. Like veins that carry human blood, channels of sap carry materials to various parts of the tree. **Xylem** transports water and nutrients from the soil up to the rest of the tree. **Phloem** is responsible for distributing sugars and food made in the leaves during photosynthesis. Sometimes the liquid a tree produces can be a terrific by-product. Maple syrup, delicious on pancakes, is derived from the sap of maple trees. But with some other sap, like the toxic concoction the sandbox tree produces, watch out. One of the most dangerous trees in the world is the manchineel, also known as the "tree of death." Its thick sap burns the skin, causing blisters and inflammation. Even standing underneath the manchineel tree can be dangerous. Rain or dew mixes with the tree's sap and creates a mixture that can cause blindness and other symptoms. But don't nix manchineel for everyone. In Florida and other tropical areas, you might see an iguana happily chomping on the tree's fruit. Go figure.

WHITE SNAKEROOT

Ageratina altissima

NATURAL HABITAT:

Eastern North America

Chapter 6
ROOT CAUSE . . . OF DEATH

Weakness. Loss of appetite. Coma, then death. Thousands of people died this way before it was apparent that white snakeroot was the cause.

Nancy Hanks Lincoln felt sick. There was an odd, bad-smelling odor in her mouth. Her stomach was upset, and she had little energy. Though it was a warm October day, her hands and feet felt cold. Nine-year-old Abraham Lincoln looked anxiously at his mother. What was the matter? Would the rest of his family get sick, too?

This went on for several days. Then, on October 5, 1818, Abraham watched as his mother died. With a heavy heart, he carved the wooden pegs that would hold his mother's coffin together.

In the early 1800s, well before he became the sixteenth president of the United States, Abraham Lincoln lived with his family in an area of Indiana called Little Pigeon Creek. Settlers had cleared stretches of forest and now widespread grasslands bordered on wooded areas dotting the countryside. Cows grazed mostly in the open fields, but when grasses dried out from lack of rain, the cows sometimes foraged near the woods. There they found a plant with clusters of white flowers. The plant wasn't their first choice, because of its bitter taste, but now and then the animals ate it, especially if there wasn't much else available. Abraham's family didn't know it at the time, but cows that ate this plant—white snakeroot—were the reason for Nancy's early death.

White snakeroot grows well in moist soil, and it prefers a spot that's partly shady. It grows 3 to 5 feet (1 to 1.5 meters) tall, a good height for hungry cattle. Innocent-looking clumps of white flowers bloom late in the season. When other flowers have come and gone, white snakeroot provides bees, butterflies, and wasps plenty of nectar. Moth caterpillars munch on the leaves, and flies lay their eggs there. While perfectly fine for these creatures, mammals beware. If horses, sheep, goats, or cows eat too many leaves and stems of white snakeroot—and when they're hungry, the plant does look appealing—it's shocking what can happen next.

White snakeroot contains a poisonous ingredient that's concentrated mostly in its roots, leaves, and stem. This toxic chemical is called tremetol. It's easy to remember this word if you think of the word *tremble*, which sounds similar. Farmers observed that after becoming ill, cattle would often tremble violently. Tremetol is so toxic that it can be fatal for humans who drink milk or eat meat from an animal that has grazed on white snakeroot. Poor Nancy Hanks Lincoln died of what people later called milk sickness after drinking milk from a neighbor's cow. And she wasn't the only one. Historians estimate that thousands of settlers died from white snakeroot poisoning in America's past.

Today, white snakeroot is common throughout many regions of the country. It's a hardy plant that

INDIGENOUS AMERICAN KNOW-HOW

Indigenous peoples of North America developed a thorough knowledge of plant properties. This information was passed down from generation to generation so people could turn to natural remedies when they had health problems. Take the stinging nettle, for example. The Cherokee made it into a tea that soothed an upset stomach. Or, to lessen back pain, the Nez Perce developed an ointment from the pitch of a ponderosa pine tree. When someone felt a headache coming on, the Chippewa made use of the roots of spreading dogbane, while the Iroquois found that field horsetail would relieve a throbbing head. As for white snakeroot, the Shawnee already knew to avoid it. Thanks to them, the settlers found out the cause of milk sickness.

Stinging nettle

grows quickly, and when conditions are right, it's a master at spreading. Narrow, tube-shaped seeds are attached to airy tails designed to catch the wind. A strong breeze lifts the parachute seeds and transfers them to a new growing spot.

White snakeroot can multiply another way, too. The plant has an underground stem called a **rhizome**. The horizontal rhizome has small growing nodes on it. From these, other stems sprout and grow upward. It might *look* like a cluster of separate white snakeroot plants are growing together, but thanks to the underground rhizome, it's all one plant. No matter which way it scatters, white snakeroot grows like a weed!

Be-LEAF It or Not

Was white snakeroot used for treating snake bites?

Maybe, at least according to some historians. But while white snakeroot does have some medicinal benefits, scientists today have not proven that it helps with venomous bites. So why was the name picked? The *white* refers to the white flowers, of course, but what about the *snakeroot* part? Was it due to twisting, snake-shaped roots? No. The rhizome does have small roots coming from it, but there's nothing snakelike about them. The only thing twisty about white snakeroot is exactly who chose its name, and why.

IT TAKES ALL SORTS

Plants, plants, and more plants. If you collected one sample of every kind of plant on Earth, you'd have around 400,000 plants. What a mess to keep track of them all . . . unless you had a system. To sort things out, scientists organize living things with **taxonomy**, the science of naming and classifying. Think of it like going to the mall. The mall contains shops for different items such as clothing, toys, and sports equipment. Enter one of these, say, a sports store, and you'll find sections based on different games—baseball, basketball, tennis, etc. From there, you'll see shelves for equipment, clothing, or specialized shoes that are further broken down into adult and children's areas. With living things, the system of categorizing goes from broad to specific, too. In the plant kingdom, there are divisions for phylum, class, order, family, genus, and species to group specific plants. A mnemonic to remember this organizational scheme might be **k**ids **p**ut **c**apes **o**n **f**urious **g**iant **s**lugs. (You can make your own mnemonic, too!)

WHITE SNAKEROOT

Kingdom: Plantae

Phylum: angiosperm

Class: dicot

Order: Asterales

Family: aster family

Genus: *Ageratina*

Species: *Ageratina altissima*

Most plants (about 90 percent) are **angiosperms**, which means they have flowers and use seeds to reproduce.

Species refers to a specific kind of plant, though there can be different varieties.

THE
SMELLY

for you
xo

GINKGO

Ginkgo biloba

NATURAL HABITAT:

China

Chapter 7
STOP AND SMELL THE GINKGO

Beautiful, yes, but for a short period each fall, seeds from these trees emit a stench worse than dog doo.

Branches snapped. The ground next to the ginkgo tree trembled. Something huge was nearby—it was *Tyrannosaurus rex*, one of the most fearsome creatures to ever inhabit the earth. But, fearsome or not, if there was ever a contest between dino and ginkgo, the tree would win—at least in the long run. Every dinosaur on Earth died during a mass extinction event sixty-five million years ago, but this plant species has been adding its aroma to the air from then until now.

Ginkgo biloba trees are the oldest type of tree known to humans. Today, scientists study fossils that show ginkgo leaves and seeds that flourished more than two hundred million years ago. While other plant species died out and were replaced by new and different

ROSES ARE RED—PLANT SYMBOLISM

Different plants represent various attributes, depending on who's talking. A red rose often signifies love, sage can refer to health and wisdom, and bamboo symbolizes strength and longevity. And the ginkgo? At the start of World War II, six ginkgo trees were growing in the center of Hiroshima, Japan. On August 6, 1945, when the US dropped an atomic bomb that battered the city's landscape, countless people, animals, and plants died. But the charred and damaged ginkgo trees were still alive! It was a symbol of hope, strength, and a better future when the trees sprouted leaves the next spring.

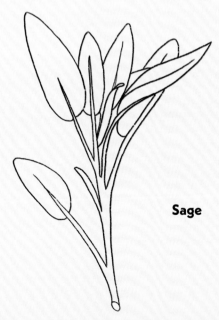

Sage

varieties, ginkgo has remained mostly unchanged throughout history. One key to its long life is its resilience. Due to the ginkgo's genetic makeup, nature can throw fungus, insect invasions, droughts, extreme weather, and even earthquakes at the tree, and chances are it will endure.

Ginkgo trees are survivors, and they're beautiful, too. Many cities around the world choose to plant them as street trees. They're a good choice for urban areas because they tolerate air pollution, excess salt from treated roads, and people walking over their roots. They also provide excellent shade. Of course, there's just one catch . . . ginkgoes produce a hold-your-nose reek during a certain time of year.

Ginkgo trees are **dioecious**, which means there are male and female varieties. Female ginkgo trees produce seeds—which are where the awful stink comes from. When the seeds ripen in the autumn, they fall to the ground. The outer seed coat begins to smell really, really bad. Some say it reminds them of vomit or like walking through a park where nobody has cleaned up after their dog. It's worse if you touch the seed coating, because the chemical that causes the odor—butyric acid—can stay on your skin for hours, no matter how much you try to scrub it off.

But what humans consider a horrible reek isn't necessarily the same for animals. Scientists speculate that some dinosaurs and now-extinct animals may have been drawn to the ginkgo stench. When they ate *Ginkgo biloba* seeds, they helped disperse the seeds through their waste.

Stinky or not, ginkgo seed nuts are eaten by people, too—they remove the outside covering first and boil, roast, or fry them, since the nuts are toxic when eaten raw (or consumed in large quantities). Especially in China, Korea, and Japan, cooks use ginkgo in tasty soups, desserts, and other dishes, such as chawanmushi (steamed egg custard) or congee (a kind of rice porridge). People have also used ginkgo products for medicinal purposes for thousands of years. So, smelly and toxic, yes, but also delicious and medically helpful!

One of the most striking things about *Ginkgo biloba* is its unique, fan-shaped leaves—dark green in the summer and brilliant yellow in the fall. The species name, *biloba*, means "two lobes," after each leaf's two lobes, or sides. And there's something unusual about the way the tree sheds these leaves each year before winter sets in. Ginkgo is a deciduous tree, meaning it drops its leaves every autumn. But while most deciduous trees lose their leaves gradually, over days or even weeks, this tree is different. Coinciding with a drop in temperature, ginkgo casts off all its leaves over just a few hours in a quick, spectacular shower of yellow. Some people like to make friendly bets about what day this will happen.

WHEN TREES LOSE IT

Deciduous trees shed their leaves every autumn. In the dry winter months, this helps the trees survive by conserving resources. Plus, in cold regions, the leaves could freeze and damage the trees if they stayed on. As soon as a deciduous tree detects less sunlight—with shorter days and longer nights—it starts the process of closing for the season. No longer in food production mode, the tree preps for the cold winter months. It develops a layer of cells that forms a fence between each leaf stem and its branch, cutting off the leaves' access to nutrients and water. The chlorophyll, which works to produce energy during the spring and summer, breaks down. Chemical changes occur. Other leaf colors—spectacular shades of yellow, orange, and red—show through as the chlorophyll's green pigment is no longer masking them. Soon, the leaves die. They drop from the tree so that in the springtime, the process of growth can begin anew.

Beautiful. Smelly. Resilient and old. Ginkgo has a long and amazing history, and not just with humans. Dinosaurs and other creatures knew the trees when the earth was young. But without these creatures distributing its seeds to new locations, ginkgo has come to depend on humans to spread to new places. At one point in Earth's history, the tree prospered naturally all over the world. Today, the only documented stand of wild ginkgo trees is located in China. What will life be like in another million years? Will ginkgo still be here to celebrate?

Be-LEAF It or Not

How did ginkgo get its name?

Ginkgo has several common names. In China, some call it the grandfather-grandchild tree, duck foot tree (the leaves do kind of look like a duck's footprint), or silver apricot, after the shape and silvery sheen of the seeds. In Japan, where the tree is also grown, the word *ginkyo* means silver apricot. In 1712, when German botanist Engelbert Kaempfer wrote a book that introduced the tree to the Western world, he made a mistake. He wrote *ginkgo* with a *g* instead of with a *y*. The mistake stuck.

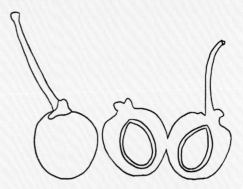

NATURE'S MEDICINE: Plants for Health

An aching head? An upset stomach? Ask a plant for help! After all, that's what people have been doing for centuries. More than four thousand years ago, in China, a medical text called *Pen Ts'ao* described which plants would help with what health issues. Then Li Shizhen (1518–1593) spent twenty-seven years writing and revising *Ben Cao Gang Mu*, an updated encyclopedia of herbal medicine that included how ginkgo improves blood circulation, helps with asthma, and has other health benefits. In 1915, the drug company Bayer began selling an over-the-counter pain medication called aspirin, and its key component was derived from a plant. Today, you can still buy aspirin at the drugstore, and scientists continue to discover new and astounding medical breakthroughs from plants. Take the Pacific yew tree, found on the northwest coast of North America. Modern researchers are excited to learn that it contains the potential cancer-fighting drug paclitaxel. The next time you get a checkup or head to the nearest pharmacy, remember the role plants play in keeping you healthy.

Yew sprig

EASTERN SKUNK CABBAGE

Symplocarpus foetidus

NATURAL HABITAT:

Eastern Canada and the United States

Chapter 8

A PAIN IN THE NOSE

Out for a run? Participate in the Skunk Cabbage Classic, in Ithaca, New York, and you'll get an unpleasant whiff approximately halfway through the course.

It's cold outside. Snow blankets the ground, and pockets of water in the swampy, wet woods are iced over. Nearby, trees stand still, their brown-gray branches bare and sleepy from winter. While the days are getting longer, flowers and shrubs will wait to grow until spring is properly underway—which makes a lot of sense. Why risk freezing to death by popping up too early? Except that not every plant has the same constraints. A small green shoot is poking up from the ground, and, curiously, the snow has melted around that exact spot.

February

March

April

June

May

July

With skunk cabbage, a plant as smelly as it sounds, there's more than meets the nose. This plant is warm! For about two weeks every year, skunk cabbage generates significant heat. Even when outside temperatures are chilly, skunk cabbage can raise the temperature of its flowers up to 70 degrees Fahrenheit (21 degrees Celsius). This ability, called **thermogenesis**, comes with lots of benefits. First, skunk cabbage gets to jump the queue. Since it begins its growing season before most other plants become active, there's less competition for sunlight, water, and nutrients from the soil.

The plant's heat also helps spread the rank smell that some say is like getting a whiff of rotting meat or skunk. And this is good? Oh, yes! Flies, gnats, and other insects like this putrid smell. As bugs come near, they

PLANT COMPETITION

When light, nutrients, and water are limited, plants find ways to curb the competition so that they can succeed. Shade-tolerant plants grow larger, thicker leaves to absorb more sunlight. **Lianas**, like English ivy or the trumpet vine, climb trees or other structures to get nearer to full sun. Skunk cabbage edges out rivals, not only by growing earlier in the season to get a jump on other plants that wait for warmer weather before they sprout, but also by growing especially deep roots to get at nutrients farther down in the soil.

English ivy

find a hood-shaped leaf that grows early in the season. This customized leaf encases a spike—the **spadix**—of yellow, petal-less flowers. The hood (the **spathe**) is open on one side so pollinators can find the flowers. Lured in close, the insects brush against pollen and transport it from one flower to another, enabling skunk cabbage to produce seeds.

But how does skunk cabbage generate the heat that helps with this process of pollination? It's not like it can exercise or throw on a jacket. Dig down! Beneath the surface of the ground, skunk cabbage has a thick, modified stem the size of a potato. This rhizome is where it stores the starches it needs to generate heat energy. Skunk cabbage taps into this stockpile of nutrients and combines it with oxygen to create some serious heat energy.

But only the aboveground plant parts get the heat. Underneath the surface, the plant doesn't produce extra warmth for the rhizome. That would take too much energy. For less cost, a mop of roots ensures the rhizome's safety. Along with doing the usual root-like things such as anchoring the plant and collecting nutrients and water from the soil, these are **contractile** roots. They grow downward, nearly 2 feet (60 centimeters) into the soil, and tighten and entrench the rhizome farther into the ground. Staying snugly underground keeps the rhizome from freezing and away from foraging animals.

As the days get longer and warmer, skunk cabbage completes the process of pollination (thanks, insects!). The spathe disintegrates, and a fruit head forms to house the seeds. Summer approaches as large, dark green leaves uncurl in a spiral pattern, like the petals of a rose. But the smell continues. When the spongy leaves are damaged or touched, move away quickly—they let off an exceptionally foul odor.

Skunk cabbage has its own

STOMATA—TIME TO EAT

To make food for a plant, leaves absorb essential sunlight along with carbon dioxide and water from their environment. To take in the carbon dioxide gas and water vapor, the leaves "breathe" through microscopic holes called **stomata** (*stoma* if you're talking about just one). Guard cells on either side of these pores decide when to open or close them. When conditions are right, they open the stomata wide. For most plants, including skunk cabbage, stomata close at night or when it's too dry outside—sealing up helps conserve water. But when stomata are open, they play a critical role in keeping the plant alive.

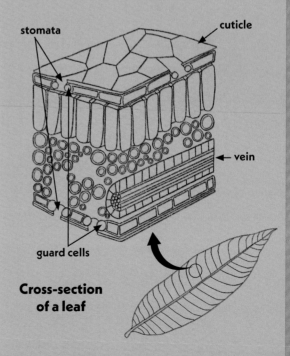

Cross-section of a leaf

pattern of growing. It may sprout early, but its foliage is gone sooner than that of many other plants. By the middle of the summer, the leaves decay. They don't dry out and become brittle, though. Full of moisture, the leaves dissolve into a leafy sludge. Is that the end for skunk cabbage? Not at all. Skunk cabbage is a **perennial**, which means that it doesn't completely die, but remains asleep—dormant—until the next growing season. Each plant lives for up to twenty years. As spring gets closer and conditions are right, it's wake-up time again.

🍃 Be-LEAF It or Not

Do animals eat skunk cabbage?

Bears wake up famished after long months of hibernation. Since skunk cabbage is one of the first plants to grow, bears, along with a few others, chomp on the young leaves. But most animals (including humans), beware! As the plant matures, so does the calcium oxalate, a sharp, crystal substance found on the leaves that can seriously irritate the tongue and throat. The crystals contain the chemical oxalic acid. To put that in perspective, oxalic acid is used to remove rust, bleach wood, or get ink stains out of laundry. The seeds, though, are fine. Squirrels, birds, and other small animals have no problems filling up on those.

ROOTING AROUND

When you walk down a sidewalk, you might notice that a chunk of cement has lifted from the rest of the walkway. What's going on? Is it the result of shoddy construction? Probably not. It could be that the roots of a nearby tree have caused the sidewalk to crack and buckle. A protective root cap on the tip of most roots acts like a shield as the root burrows through rough, rocky soil—or against a human-made structure like a wall or sidewalk. Never underestimate the power of a root! Roots have three main jobs. They make sure the plant stays put in windy conditions or loose soil. (The contractile roots of skunk cabbage, which usually grows in loose, marshy soil, take that to a whole new level by providing a deep anchor.) Next, roots collect water and minerals—especially nitrogen, phosphorus, and potassium—from the soil to feed to the rest of the plant. Roots also store energy. In the winter months when there's less sunlight, a plant might be dormant. During this time, roots provide stored energy for the plant to stay alive. But not all roots look or act the same. When you think of roots, you think underground, right? Not always—some plants, especially climbing plants, grow **aerial roots**. These are aboveground roots that serve the same purpose as their belowground cousins.

DEAD HORSE ARUM

Helicodiceros muscivorus

NATURAL HABITAT:

Mediterranean islands of
Corsica, Sardinia, and the
Balearic Islands

Chapter 9
OF CORPSE IT SMELLS BAD

Dead horse arum pretends to be a
dead animal—and it's good at it.

Ah, flowers! Brilliant, jewel-colored blossoms framed by fresh foliage. Inhale their sweet-smelling perfume that wafts through the air. Gift them for a birthday or special occasion. Roses, orchids, irises, magnolias . . . All flowers are beautiful, right?

Not quite. Imagine the opposite and you've got the dead horse arum.

A smell like rotting flesh? Check.

A meat-colored modified leaf? Check.

A hairy tail? Check.

This plant is definitely NOT something you'd want in a vase in your house. An expert in the ways of disguise, dead horse arum looks and smells like a rotting carcass—roadkill on steroids. The bogus—and amazing—corpse pretense is all an elaborate ruse that tempts certain insects to draw near so they can help with pollination. Luckily for humans, dead horse arum's stinky bloom lasts only a couple of days. But for those two days, oh, the smell!

You can find dead horse arum growing naturally among limestone and granite on the rocky coastal clifftops of several Mediterranean islands. Around the world, it's a novelty in various greenhouses and botanical gardens, too. The plant starts off innocently enough. First come long, arrow-shaped leaves that grow in a cluster. When dead horse arum blooms, a customized leaf, the spathe, sprouts up. The spathe uncurls and reveals a hairy, meat-colored surface. This is the first deception. Next is a long, narrow knob that looks a lot like a tail. It bristles with short plant hairs. This tail-looking part lies along the spathe and reaches into a dark opening where the flower is housed. So far, so good. But dead horse arum isn't done yet.

Red columbine

COLOR CONNECTION

Flowers are attrac*tive*, but more importantly, they are attracto*rs*. Many need insects, birds, or other animals to help them with pollination. Color is one way that flowers entice various creatures to swing by. For instance, hummingbirds often prefer red and pink flowers. For a cardinal flower or red columbine, the long, narrow beak of a hummingbird is perfect for reaching inside the tapering petals. Most bees are drawn to blue, purple, or yellow flowers. Many night-blooming flowers are white, helping pollinators locate them when there's little light. And what about the meaty-colored spathe of the dead horse arum? Flies *like* feasting on dead animals, so when a plant mimics the colors of a decaying carcass, the flies are all in.

WHEN SMELL MAKES SENSE

A plant's aroma (or stench) is tailored to attract (or repel) certain animals. Some plants, such as magnolia or lavender, entice pollinators with sweet, sugary perfumes. And while this appeals to many kinds of birds, bees, and/or butterflies, other insects, such as beetles and flies, prefer a different smell. For them, the reek of a plant like dead horse arum is like the smell of a delicious dinner for us. Another example is the valerian plant, whose aroma might remind you of sweaty gym socks. While bees and butterflies frequently swing by this flower, deer avoid the gym-socky smell, thus saving the plant from being overeaten.

Lavender

Dead horse arum, like some of its close relatives, can generate heat. By making the so-called tail warm and smelly, the plant fools blowflies into thinking that it is a real dead animal. And in fact, some of the chemicals in the dead horse arum's enticing "perfume" are present in actual rotting meat. Yum for the blowflies! Plus, it seems like a great place to lay their eggs. (But sadly, if a fly does attempt to lay its eggs there, the maggots won't survive.)

The scheme to entice insects is successful when flies crawl inside dead horse arum's spathe to the spadix, the column of tiny male and female flowers. Here the flies rub up against the flowers' sticky pollen. If the insects can carry this pollen to other dead horse arum plants, they'll help those plants reproduce.

After the fly crawls inside the opening at the end of the spathe, it moves down the column to the female flowers. Any pollen the insect's already carrying from other dead horse arum plants brushes off and onto these flowers. This takes some time, and dead horse arum wants to be sure the flies get the job done right. The solution? Thick spikes located just above the shaft of female flowers move into place and block the exit, temporarily trapping the flies inside.

Within a few hours, dead horse arum is done caging the flies. Its flowers have collected the pollen from the insects' bodies. The male section of the flowering column has produced new pollen. Soon, the spikes wilt and the jail cell opens. The flies are free to go . . . but not before brushing against

YOU HELP ME AND I'LL HELP YOU

Sometimes in nature, the feeling's mutual. Plants rely on insects, birds, and other animals to help with pollination. In turn, the plant might provide nourishment like nectar, fruit, or seeds. In the case of dead horse arum, greenish-brown Balearic lizards help themselves—and the plant. A lizard hears the buzzing insects caught inside the spadix and goes in to investigate. Eating its fill of flies, it also chows down on seeds from the plant. Later, it poops these out, helping the seeds find a new place to sprout. Thank you, plant, and thank you, lizard!

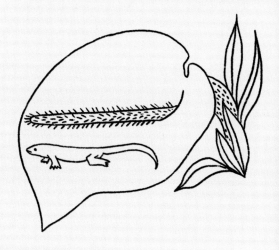

this new batch of pollen, which they'll carry to a different plant. Success! For the plant, it's an excellent system for gathering and dispensing pollen.

Dead horse arum may seem like one of the smelliest, strangest plants on the planet. It's famously weird, so maybe your local botanical garden has one. But if you do visit the plant and it's flowering, pinch your nose tightly, and try not to breathe.

🍃 Be-LEAF It or Not

What other odd arums are in the family?

There's more than one plant from the arum family that stinks. Solomon's lily, native to the Middle East, smells yeasty and attracts vinegar flies. Some people say that the innocent-sounding lords-and-ladies plant reeks of urine. The largest member of the family—and the stinkiest—is titan arum, native to western Sumatra, in Indonesia. The flowering part alone (the spadix) of titan arum can be 10 feet (3 meters) tall. When this plant blooms once every four to ten years, it's enormous—and the stench! BLECH.

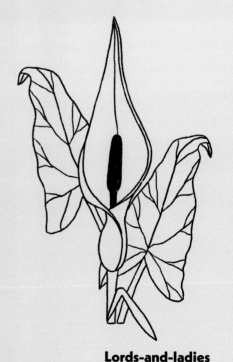

Lords-and-ladies

WHEN PLANTS COMMUNICATE

Incoming! Hungry aphids descend on a bean plant and begin their assault. Does the bean plant just sit there and take it? Definitely not! It warns the rest of the plant—and calls in reinforcements. The plant releases a chemical signal that prompts the rest of the plant to boost security by producing an anti-aphid bug repellent. The bean plant also calls on wasps—another chemical signal does the trick—that come in to attack the aphids. Of course, from the wasps' perspective, they're not there to fight; it's just mealtime. Like bean plants, dead horse arum relies on airborne chemicals (in its case, to draw pollinators close by imitating the odor of decay). But scientists have found that plants can send messages through air *or* soil. Some plants communicate underground with the assistance of fungi, threadlike organisms that can help plants collect water and minerals. Plants can also use these tiny pathways to make chemical contact with other vegetation. Of course, plant talk isn't always cooperative. Knapweed's roots release toxins engineered to kill off their competition. Maybe plants don't go about things the way a human would, but scientists agree: plant communication is real!

THE
EXCEPTIONALLY
STRANGE

VENUS FLYTRAP

Dionaea muscipula

NATURAL HABITAT:

Coastal plains of North and South Carolina

Chapter 10
COME A LITTLE CLOSER

When hunger strikes, the Venus flytrap goes for a meat dish.

Closer. Closer . . . A plump spider is minding its own business as it climbs over a Venus flytrap plant. But it's dinnertime, and if this plant had a stomach, it would be growling. *That's it, nearly there . . .* Now the spider is crawling across the open leaf. It brushes against the first trigger hair, but the Venus flytrap isn't yet sure. Then one of the spider's legs touches a second trigger hair, and *SNAP!* In less than a second, the plant slams both lobes of its leaf closed, ensnaring the spider. *Gotcha!*

Welcome to one of the world's most amazing meat-eaters. It's no shark or lion, but the Venus flytrap is just as lethal, only on a smaller scale. While most plants get the nutrients they need from soil, Venus flytraps grow naturally in wet, boggy areas where the soil doesn't provide enough necessary nutrients such as nitrogen and phosphorus. No problem. The Venus flytrap supplements its diet from another source: insect soup.

CARNIVOROUS PLANT CLUB

Carnivorous—or meat-eating—plants like the Venus flytrap rely on additional nutrients from living things in order to survive. These types of plants grow on every continent except Antarctica, and there are more than six hundred individual species. In terms of scale, a penny-size sundew is among the smallest of the carnivorous plants. It's about as big as the tip of your finger. The largest is *Nepenthes rajah*, which is native to Malaysian Borneo. This pitcher-shaped plant has a foot-long (30-centimeter) opening and is filled with nearly 1 gallon (3.5 liters) of water. While *Nepenthes rajah* focuses mostly on ants, occasionally it will trap and digest larger animals such as frogs, lizards, and small rodents. With tree shrews, the plant does things a little differently. Sometimes when a tree shrew perches on the plant to chow down on some nectar, it poops inside the opening. But no worries—for *Nepenthes rajah*, this shrew-poo is a good thing: free nitrogen!

The Venus flytrap is a carnivorous plant of medium size. Its clamshell-shaped leaf traps are red and green to lure certain insects close, and they grow low to the ground in a cluster of about six per plant. Each leaf trap is made up of two lobes, each with fifteen to twenty spines along its edge. In response to being touched, the lobes clasp shut in a movement called **thigmonasty**. At first, the Venus flytrap's spines don't overlap completely. Slightly open, they form the bars of an insect cage. There's a reason for this. If a Venus flytrap accidentally captures an insect that's too small, the openings allow the insect to fly away. When a Venus flytrap catches dinner, it wants to make sure it's worthwhile.

The Venus flytrap has helpful **adaptations** to ensure the process works well. What if the trap

CATCHING ON WITH CARNIVOROUS PLANTS— TYPES OF TRAPS

Plants like the Venus flytrap and the waterwheel plant have snap traps. When insects get close—WHOOSH—leaves lock around them so they can't escape. Other carnivorous plants use different mechanisms for catching prey. A sundew plant has tentacles topped with droplets that look like water as they glisten in the sun. While this might look pretty—and tempting—it's a sticky situation for an insect. The sundew plant uses this adhesive trap to capture its next meal. Pitfall traps are no less deadly. A pitcher plant ensnares its prey with modified leaves that are filled with liquid. This plant entices insects (and sometimes larger animals) to explore its pitcher-shaped leaf, but when they slip down inside, slick sides mean there's no escape. They drown in a pool of watery digestive fluids. A snare trap, like that of the corkscrew plant, has a similar adaptation. It's easy for prey to enter, but with the plant's strategically placed hairs, it's nearly impossible to exit. Finally, bladderwort creates a mini suction device to vacuum its prey inside. Time to eat!

snapped shut every time a drop of rain splashed down or a twig blew past? That would be a huge waste of energy. Introducing two-time trigger hairs. Each lobe typically has three sensitive bristles, called **trichomes**, spaced along the surface. An insect must touch at least two bristles within twenty seconds for the trap to slam closed. When this happens, within an hour or so, the plant oozes digestive juices that slowly eat away at the new meal. The process can take up to several days, but once the Venus flytrap has absorbed all the essential nutrients it needs, it opens and—POP—releases the empty insect shell.

The meat-trapping leaves of the Venus flytrap aren't the only interesting thing about this plant. From spring to early summer each year, the plant produces a cluster of white flowers. They help the

Venus flytrap reproduce. When insects, mostly sweat bees and certain beetles, come looking for nectar, pollen temporarily sticks to their bodies. They fly from flower to flower. When the pollen falls off, the insects unintentionally transfer it from one part of the flower called the **stamen** to another part called the **pistil**. But how does the Venus flytrap keep from accidentally eating these helpful insects? It's a predator-prey conundrum. For starters, the flowers grow on top of a very long stem, up to 14 inches (36 centimeters) long. By keeping far away from the "mouth" of the plant, pollinators stay safe (and can continue doing their job). Scientists think that color and smell have something to do with it, too. The insects attracted to the white flowers are different from those who go for the red and green of the leaf traps.

PLANTS IN PERIL

When cities, industry, and large farms take over certain regions, native plants are often squeezed out. To counteract this issue, some countries have set aside nature preserves where it's illegal to disturb the plants and animals that live there. Even still, plenty of plants are in trouble—some are in danger of becoming extinct. And when people take a plant from its natural habitat and sow it somewhere else, without proper management the plant can become an invasive species. This means that it can take over, upsetting the balance of plant and animal life that was there first. Other problems for plants include increased pollution and a changing climate. When temperatures vary too much from normal levels, it can cause plant distress. Climate change can also affect precipitation. With too little rain—or too much—plants may not survive. The bottom line: It's up to everyone to take care of our natural world.

To many people, the Venus flytrap is a celebrity plant. But fame can have its disadvantages. Loss of habitat and overcollecting have put the plant in danger of dying out. Today it's against the law to take Venus fly-trap plants from the wild. People who do can be fined or even sent to jail. Buyers beware: purchase Venus flytraps from a reputable source and learn how to lovingly take care of these talented plants.

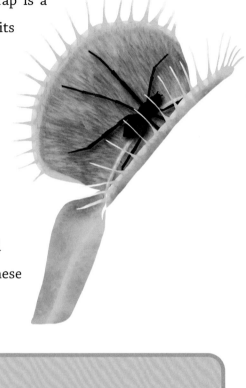

🌿 Be-LEAF It or Not

Does the Venus flytrap eat mostly flies?

Not even close. A Venus flytrap supplements the nutrients it pulls from the soil with insects, but despite the name, flies don't rank #1. More than 60 percent of the plant's meat diet is not flies but ants and spiders. Beetles and grasshoppers make up around 10 percent each. And flies? Only about 5 percent.

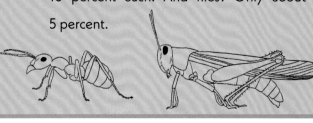

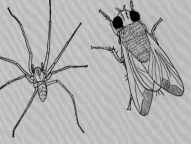

BANKING ON SEEDS FOR THE FUTURE

Take a trip to a bank vault. It's underground and well protected. Inside is wealth unimaginable, a treasure trove of billions of . . . seeds. This is Svalbard Global Seed Vault, located in Norway. It's nicknamed the "doomsday vault," and its purpose is to resupply seeds when plants are destroyed through human-made or natural disasters. Saving plants for the future is so critical that there are hundreds of seed banks scattered around the world. These include Mamudpur Nayakrishi Seed Hut in Bangladesh, Haritha Udana in Sri Lanka, and the Cherokee Nation Seed Bank in the United States, where people store plants with historical and cultural importance. The largest seed bank in the world is the Millennium Seed Bank in Sussex, England. It houses a diverse collection of preserved seeds, a staggering fifty thousand species from approximately two hundred countries and territories. When plants are threatened by habitat loss or a changing climate, the global seed banks ensure that the species survives.

SEED BATCH 1

SEED BATCH 3

SEED BATCH 2

Chapter 11

A STONE ...
OR PLANT?

Watch where you're stepping
in the oldest desert on Earth—
because those rocks? They may not
be rocks.

Yum! *Munch!* Many plants are delicious and a great source of nutrition. But in nature, it's all about balance. If you're a plant, you might be willing to share, but you don't want animals to eat you out of existence. What's a plant to do when there's a hungry herbivore nearby? Lithops hides in plain sight.

Find lithops—or at least try to—in extremely dry areas of southern Africa. But be careful where you walk because these plants take camouflage to a whole new level. Lithops has two plump leaves that look like stones. The disguise fools people and animals, too. With creatures such as beetles, elephant shrews, and cape ground squirrels constantly on the lookout for food and water, it's a smart way to not get eaten.

There are approximately 145 kinds of lithops that vary in size, texture, and color. The largest are up to 2 inches (5 centimeters) wide, but most are smaller. Some are smooth, while others have a more pebbled surface. The pattern and colors vary depending on the surrounding environment— these plants pick the right disguise for where they live.

Despite their differences, various species of lithops have several things in common. For one, they keep a low profile. Like an iceberg in the middle of the sea, most of the plant is underground. This helps the plant regulate heat since the desert environment can swing hot or cold. At its hottest, it might climb to a blistering 120 degrees Fahrenheit (49 degrees Celsius). At this temperature, chocolate, gummy candies, and even crayons melt. But it's not

CLEVER ABOUT CAMOUFLAGE

Have you ever noticed how animals blend in? An Arctic fox, brown in the summer, turns white in the winter. A stick insect looks like . . . a stick. Plants have incredible disguises, too. To survive animals preying on them, *Corydalis hemidicentra* leaves merge into their surroundings by mimicking the gray color of the surrounding rock. Others use fake information. Elephant ears—*Caladium steudneriifolium*—dissuade moths from eating their leaves by producing a pattern of whitish lines that make it seem like the insects have already been there and chowed down. Members of the *Axinaea* flower genus from Central and South America dupe birds with stamens that look like delicious berries. Free lunch! But when birds take a peck, air squeezes from the plant, and a blast of pollen lands on the bird's beak and head. Perfect—the birds fly the pollen to another flower. See? Lithops isn't the only one with a secret.

always blazing hot. During colder parts of the year, when the temperature dips significantly at night, being mostly underground keeps lithops warm. It's like having a snug dirt sleeping bag.

Lithops are **xerophytes**, plants that survive with almost no rain. Those that live along coastal areas rely on fog to get the moisture they need. Farther inland, lithops can last for months without rain if necessary. During the most intense periods of drought, the plant hunkers down. It shrivels and shrinks lower into the ground, where it waits for better conditions. That way, the water it does have stored won't evaporate.

With just the top of the leaves above ground, the rest of lithops is a rounded cone shape with tapering, vertical roots trailing several inches into the soil. The two visible leaves are mostly flat and plump, with a gap between the two leaf halves. With the bulk of the plant away from the sun, leaf "windows" are another excellent adaptation. These translucent membranes on the surface of the leaves

welcome sunlight in so that it can reach deep into the plant where photosynthesis—food production—occurs. There's just one problem: at times, the sunshine can be *too* intense. Fortunately for lithops, it has **non-photochemical quenching**, which is sort of like sunscreen. It helps protect against too many of the sun's harmful rays by diffusing the light when it gets to be too much.

Just because something looks like a rock, it doesn't mean it has to act like a rock. After three years, lithops produces a flower. The flower, usually white, yellow, or pale orange, springs up between the two leaves. It opens in the afternoon and closes by sunset. Attracted by the color and scent, insects buzz over and help transfer pollen so the plant can produce seeds.

THE ISSUE WITH THE TISSUE

Take a trek into a desert or through one of Earth's drier regions, and you'll likely come across a succulent. Lithops are succulents—so are cactuses. These plants are named after the Latin word *sucus*, which means "juice" or "sap." They have plump, fleshy tissues (leaves, stem, roots), which store what little water there is and keep the plant from drying out. Succulents can often go for long periods of time without rain or moisture in the air. Coming in a wide variety of colors and with various features, most succulents have deep or broadly reaching roots and a hairy, waxy, or thorny outer surface. This thick surface keeps too much water from evaporating away from the plant.

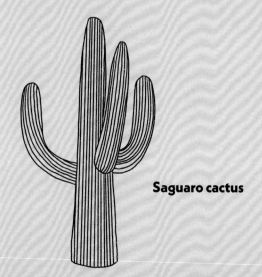

Saguaro cactus

After being pollinated, the flowers die and a seedpod grows, containing a couple hundred tiny seeds. Next is a lesson in patience. The lithops seedpod needs moisture to open. When rain finally comes, it splashes the seeds away from the parent plant. With the right conditions, the seeds grow into brand-new lithops.

People are still discovering more varieties of lithops. In 2006, a man named Tok Schoeman found a sample that nobody had officially recognized. He named it *Lithops amicorum*, which means "in honor of friends."

Small, sure. But with exceptional adaptations? Absolutely. Carve this sentence in stone: Lithops are one of the most remarkable plants on Earth.

Be-LEAF It or Not

What does lithops's name mean?

Living stone, stoneface, pebble plant . . . Some people even lovingly call lithops the butt plant because of its shape. In South Africa, the Afrikaans nickname for it is *skaappootjie* or *beeskloutjie*, meaning "sheep hoof" or "cattle hoof." But the rocklike colors and shape of lithops give this plant its scientific name. The official name was adopted in 1922 from the Greek words *lithos*, meaning "stone," and *opsis*, meaning "like."

EXTREMOPHILES

Imagine if sand—and no water—stretched for as far as you could see. How could any plant survive in such harsh conditions? Introducing: **extremophiles**. These, like lithops, are living things that thrive in extreme environments. They include desert plants, which are experts at conserving water and heat. Along with lithops in the Namib Desert is *Welwitschia*, another southwestern African plant treasure. With only two leathery leaves, the plant lives to be hundreds of years old, despite the fact that there are no water sources within miles. It relies on dew and fog to stay alive.

Then there are extremophiles in places where there's plenty of water . . . but it's all frozen. Even in Antarctica, lichens, fungi, algae, and moss prosper. Travel next to the opposite pole where the Arctic is a frozen wasteland—not! Out of all the flowering plants, purple saxifrage grows the farthest north. To protect against the Arctic cold, tiny hairs on its leaves trap air, the same way wearing many layers of clothing keeps you warm. But purple saxifrage also needs to guard against intense winds that would tear and devastate other plants. The answer? Low and slow. It sticks to spaces between rocks that are close to the ground and away from the bulk of the wind. And unhurried growth—similar to lithops—means it doesn't use a lot of energy, either, which is another good way to stay alive.

Chapter 12
IF IT LOOKS LIKE A DUCK . . .

Beak, wings, and body—you can almost imagine this tiny flower taking flight.

There's an old saying that goes like this: If it looks like a duck, swims like a duck, and quacks like a duck, then it probably *is* a duck. This suggests that if something seems like a certain thing, it probably is that thing. But not so fast! The flying-duck orchid is a delicate flower that looks a lot like a duck in motion—at least to us humans.

When it's time to go duck hunting, look carefully (for the flying duck *orchid*, of course). It's a **terrestrial** plant, meaning it grows from the ground (versus in the water or on another plant such as a tree). It prefers sandy, gravelly soil where water drains fast. The orchid flowers themselves are tiny, less than an inch (1–2 centimeters) long. You'll usually find two or three blooms perched on top of a wiry, 8- to 20-inch (20- to 50-centimeter) stem that's nestled among grasses and shrubs. But don't expect to find this plant just anywhere. It's a picky eater and relies on a fungus found only in woody areas of Australia where eucalyptus trees grow.

The flying-duck orchid might look like a duck to humans, but not so to its pollinator, the sawfly. The orchid attracts male sawflies by mimicking the colors and scent of a female sawfly. The rounded head and beak of the flower—the **labellum**—is a kind of petal platform where the sawfly lands when looking for a mate. Two "wings" protrude from the side. These two modified leaves, known as **sepals**, plus a third lower down support the flower.

MEET THE FAMILY

With more than twenty-eight thousand species, Orchidaceae—members of the orchid family—live on every continent but Antarctica. Fossil evidence suggests that orchid ancestors were alive about 120 million years ago. As far as today's relatives go, orchids can be big or small. One of the largest species is *Grammatophyllum speciosum*. Growing in a clump that weighs up to 4,400 pounds (2,000 kilograms), as heavy as a rhinoceros, this grandma can be found in Singapore, where it's celebrated as the country's national flower. Compare that to the tiniest orchids, such as the *Platystele*, which has blooms about as wide as the sharpened tip of a crayon. Discovered in Ecuador, it has petals that are one cell thick and impossible to see without major magnification. Within that size range are many more eccentric family members. These include the naked-man orchid, tiger's-mouth orchid, dove orchid, and ghost orchid. With such odd-ball names, there's a lot to love about orchids.

G. *speciosum* orchid

When a male sawfly swoops by to make friends, *ZAP!* The top part of the flower closes over the insect, trapping it inside. Once a package of pollen—called a **pollinium**—sticks to the sawfly, the "duck" opens and lets it go. Bringing the bundle of pollen with it, the insect tries again on another sawfly-looking, sawfly-smelling orchid. This time it releases the pollen it's carrying. The second plant uses this pollen to start the process of reproducing by creating seeds for new plants.

With so many varieties, orchids have a massive list of differences—color, size, shape, smell, and more. But they have lots of things in common, too. For one, orchids have tiny seeds. The flying-duck orchid is no exception. After it blooms from about September to January each year, the plant produces hard, compact capsules that contain up to five hundred minuscule seeds each. The pod opens and the dust-like seeds fall to the ground. Unlike most flower seeds, though, there is no stored food inside the flying-duck orchid seed coat. This seed, if it germinates at all, must rely on the particular fungi in the soil to provide the necessary nutrients to grow. This **symbiotic relationship**—a connection between two living things that benefits them both—makes it exceptionally difficult for people to cultivate their own flying-duck orchids in other parts of the world.

Maybe your next flower arrangement won't have a flying-duck orchid, but plenty of other orchids that can be grown outside their native habitat show up internationally at various festivals and events. They're beautiful

Bee orchid

TRICKS AND TRAPS

Many orchids, like the flying-duck orchid, have adaptations to attract a specific kind of insect to help them with pollination. By concentrating on just one or a few species of insects, they sideline some of the competition. The monkey-face orchid (which really does look like a monkey's face) targets fungus gnats by mimicking a local kind of mushroom that the gnats feast on. A bee orchid looks and smells like a female bee. Male bees zoom in and get covered in pollen before they realize they've been duped. Like the relationship that the flying-duck orchid has with sawflies, each of these orchids gets free pollen transfer—though sometimes it costs them a little nectar.

and unusual, and lots have spectacular smells that can be extracted and used in recipes or for perfume. (Guess what the vanilla orchid is used for? Found in Mexico and Central America, this orchid is where baking vanilla comes from.)

It's easy to see why people are obsessed with orchids!

Be-LEAF It or Not

Are all orchids terrestrial; that is, do they grow only from the ground?

Not at all. Some orchids are **epiphytes**, which means they grow on another plant, usually a tree where there's more access to the sun. But they're not **parasites**—that is, they don't steal nutrients from their host. Instead, with free-hanging roots, they collect nutrients and water from the air. Many orchids are terrestrial, though, like the flying-duck orchid. One of the weirdest terrestrial orchids is *Rhizanthella gardneri*, the western underground orchid. It can't photosynthesize, so it helps itself to all the nutrients it needs from a fungus found in Australia. To this parasitic plant, all that energy spent making food is a waste when you can hijack someone else's supplies.

"Parasitic plants are fascinating because they overturn almost everything that defines a plant. Many parasitic plants do not perform photosynthesis (thus not green) and have highly unusual appearances. Some of them live entirely inside the host and only emerge to make seeds—a very sci-fi type of story." —*Dr. Liming Cai, University of Texas*

PLANTS IN HIGH PLACES

The middle of the desert. Underwater. On top of mountains. Plants grow in all kinds of harsh environments on Earth. But have scientists ever tried rocketing plants (including orchids) past Earth? Yes! Both China and Russia have sent orchids to space. NASA has done a lot of space plant experimentation, too. In all cases, scientists have found that growing plants off-planet requires a lot of care. Though today's astronauts who work on the International Space Station (ISS) rely on supply vessels to deliver food and essential supplies, they've also been experimenting with growing various plants such as lettuce, zinnia flowers, and Chinese cabbage. Success! Since 2015, American astronauts have been eating crops grown in space. Aboard the ISS, you can meet Veggie (Vegetable Production System). In this suitcase-size greenhouse, scientists must work out several basic challenges. The plants there receive artificial light since they aren't exposed to sunlight. To combat microgravity, seeds are planted in clay or gel instead of soil. And special systems ensure that water and nutrients get to the plant instead of simply floating away. While this particular experimental station requires human care, the Advanced Plant Habitat (APH) is fully automated. In either habitat, in space every plant is treated like a VIP—that is, a very important plant.

Glossary

adaptation: a feature developed by a plant or other organism to ensure its survival in a specific environment

aerial roots: located above ground, they collect nutrients and water from the air and help anchor the plant onto a tree or other structure

angiosperm: a flowering plant that produces seeds and fruit

anther: part of the stamen of a flower; this is where pollen is located

aril: a covering around certain seeds

biomimicry: when inspiration from nature helps people solve real-world problems

blade: the large and usually flat surface of a leaf that is attached to a stalk

bract: a modified leaf that typically protects a flower bud

chlorophyll: a green substance found in leaves that uses energy from the sun to help a plant produce its own food

cone: a protective structure where some trees store their seeds

conifer: a kind of tree, usually an evergreen, that has cones and needle-shaped or scaly leaves

contractile roots: these tighten or draw together to pull the plant farther into the soil

cross-pollination: when pollen is carried from one flower to another to enable reproduction

deciduous tree: a kind of tree that drops its leaves every autumn and grows new leaves the following spring

dehiscence: when a mature plant splits open naturally to release contents such as seeds or pollen

dendrochronology: the study of the pattern of growth rings on a tree

dicot: a flowering plant that has two seed leaves

dioecious: when male reproductive organs are in one variety and female reproductive organs are in another variety of the same species

embryo: the part of a seed that will grow into a plant

epiphyte: a plant that's not a parasite but grows on another structure like a tree or fence

extremophiles: plants or other organisms that live in challenging environments

genus: a category for organizing species that share certain similar characteristics

labellum: a distinct, modified petal that forms a lip or platform

liana: a woody vine that grows up a tree and maintains roots in the ground

midrib: the main, usually central vein of a leaf

nectar: a sweet liquid produced by plants

non-photochemical quenching: the ability of a plant to diffuse excess energy from too much sun

ovary: the place where seeds develop after pollination occurs

parasite: a plant or other organism that siphons off nutrients from another living thing instead of collecting its own

perennial: a plant that has a life cycle of more than one year

petiole: the stalk of a leaf

phloem: a system that carries food made by photosynthesis in a plant's leaves to other parts of the plant

photosynthesis: the process by which plants use sunlight, water, and carbon dioxide to create their own food

pistil: the female reproductive organs of a flower

pollen: a dusty substance produced by a flower that begins the process of creating a seed

pollinium (pl. pollinia): a distinct package of pollen versus individual pollen grains

rhizome: an underground stem that usually grows horizontally

self-pollination: the transfer of pollen on a single plant from where it's produced to where it's needed to begin the process of reproduction

sepal: a modified leaf found on the outermost part of a flower

spadix: a spike of flowers

spathe: a covering that surrounds one or more flowers or a spadix

stamen: the male reproductive organs of a flower

stigma: the part of a flower that receives pollen needed for the process of seed development

stoma (pl. stomata): microscopic holes on a leaf and stem that allow a plant to "breathe in" carbon dioxide and "breathe out" oxygen

symbiotic relationship: a bond between two organisms that benefits both

taxonomy: a way to name and organize organisms, including plants

terrestrial: relating to the earth; for a plant, this means it grows from the ground

thermogenesis: a plant's ability to generate heat

thigmonasty: a plant's ability to physically respond when touched

trichomes: sensitive bristle hairs located on a plant

xerophyte: a plant that survives with very little water

xylem: a system that brings water and nutrients from the roots to the rest of the plant

Source Notes

p. 41: "Plants are amazing organisms . . . etc., etc.!!": Dr. Tanisha Williams, "Tanisha Williams: Botanist and Founder of Black Botanists Week," *Nature* (blog), PBS, February 11, 2021, accessed August 7, 2022, https://www.pbs.org/wnet /nature/blog/tanisha-williams/.

p. 122: "Parasitic plants . . . sci-fi type of story": Dr. Liming Cai (postdoctoral researcher at the University of Texas, Austin), interview with the author, September 27, 2022.

Select Bibliography

Aaseng, Nathan. *Killer Carnivorous Plants*. New York: Enslow Publishing, 2019.

Crowley, Dan, and Douglas Justice. *The Lives of Leaves: 50 Leaves, What They Mean, and What They Mean to Us*. London: Two Roads (Hachette UK), 2021.

Hoare, Ben, and Kaley McKean (illustrator). *The Secret World of Plants: Tales of More than 100 Remarkable Flowers, Trees, and Seeds*. New York: DK Children, 2022.

Ignotofsky, Rachel. *What's Inside a Flower? And Other Questions about Science and Nature*. New York: Dragonfly Books, 2023.

Jenkins, Martin, and James Brown (illustrator). *A World of Plants*. Somerville, MA: Candlewick Studio, 2021.

Montgomery, Beronda L. *Lessons from Plants*. Cambridge, MA: Harvard University Press, 2021.

Stewart, Amy, with Briony Morrow-Cribbs (etchings) and Jonathon Rosen (illustrations). *Wicked Plants: The Weed That Killed Lincoln's Mother and Other Botanical Atrocities*. Chapel Hill, NC: Algonquin Books, 2009.

Thorogood, Chris. *Weird Plants*. Royal Botanical Gardens, Kew, England: Kew Publishing, 2018.

Willis, Kathy, and Katie Scott (illustrator). *Welcome to the Museum: Botanicum*. Somerville, MA: Big Picture Press, 2017.

Acknowledgments

At the end of any worthy project (and I learned so much and had such joy with this one), there's a time to reflect on all the excellent help I received. I could not have done this without James McGowan or my brilliant and fun editor, Olivia Swomley, and the rest of the amazing MIT Kids Press team. I'm thrilled to be paired with the oh-so-talented Zoë Ingram and her incredible art. Lucky for this book! Next is my community of writers and illustrators who expand my brain (and love) every day by contributing their thoughts and support. Thank you especially to Hena Khan, Laura Gehl, Joan Waites, and so many others. Thank you, too, for the blessing of my incredibly supportive family, Rich, and our wonderful kids. My heart is full.

Index

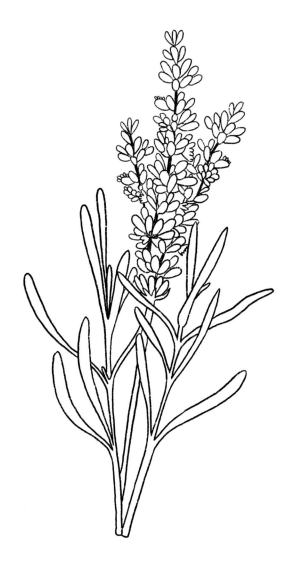

Ann McCallum Staats is the author of numerous children's books, including *Eat Your Science Homework*, a Junior Library Guild Selection, as well as the rest of the Eat Your Homework series; *The Secret Life of Math*, which won the *Foreword Reviews* Book of the Year Gold Award; and *High Flyers: 15 Inspiring Women Aviators and Astronauts*. She has a master's degree in education and lives in Virginia with her family.

Zoë Ingram is an artist, designer, and author. With an honors degree in industrial design for textiles and a career in graphic design and the creative arts spanning over twenty years, she primarily works with mixed media and digital applications, often combining both traditional and digital techniques. You'll find her work on fabric, stationery, greeting cards, magazines, books, and home decor products. She lives in Edinburgh, Scotland.

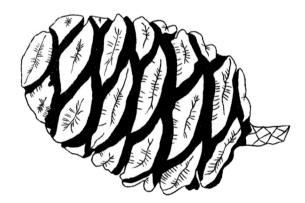